V&A Pattern
William Morris
and Morris & Co.

V&A Publishing

V&A Pattern
William Morris
and Morris & Co.

First published by V&A Publishing, 2009
V&A Publishing
Victoria and Albert Museum
South Kensington
London SW7 2RL

ISBN 978 1 851 77584 2
Library of Congress Control Number 2009923087

10 9 8 7 6 5 4 3
2013 2012 2011

A catalogue record for this book is available
from the British Library.

Design: Rose

Front cover (A):
William Morris/Morris & Co.
Fruit wallpaper. Block-printed paper. UK, 1866 (V&A: E.3711–1927)
Pages 2–3 (B):
John Henry Dearle/Morris & Co.
Golden Lily wallpaper. Block-printed paper. UK, 1897 (V&A: E.1407–1979)
Page 6 (C):
William Morris/Morris & Co.
Sunflower wallpaper. Block-printed paper. UK, 1879 (V&A: E.513–1919)
Page 11 (D):
William Morris/Morris & Co.
Wild Tulip wallpaper. Block-printed paper. UK, 1884 (V&A: E.538–1919)
Pages 78–9 (E):
John Henry Dearle/Morris & Co.
Harebell wallpaper. Block-printed paper. UK, 1911 (V&A: E.1420–1979)

Letters in (brackets) refer to the file name of the images on the
accompanying disc. Where different colourways of patterns
are shown, a cross reference is given in the caption. Due to the
nature of the originals, it has not always been possible to match
the repeats exactly.

Printed in China

V&A Publishing

Supporting the world's leading
museum of art and design,
the Victoria and Albert
Museum, London

V&A Pattern

Each *V&A Pattern* book is an introduction to the Victoria and Albert Museum's extraordinarily diverse design archives. The museum has more than three million designs for textiles, decorations, wallpapers and prints; some well-known, others less so. This series explores pattern-making in all its forms, across the world and through the centuries. The books are intended to be both beautiful and useful – showing patterns to enjoy in their own right and as inspiration for new design.

V&A Pattern presents the greatest names and styles in design, while also highlighting the work of anonymous draughtsmen and designers, often working unacknowledged in workshops, studios and factories, and responsible for designs of aesthetic originality and technical virtuosity. Many of the most interesting and imaginative designs are seen too rarely. *V&A Pattern* gathers hidden treasures – from pattern books, swatch books, company archives, design records and catalogues – to form a fascinating introduction to the variety and beauty of pattern at the V&A.

The compact disc at the back of each book invites you to appreciate the ingenuity of the designs, and the endless possibilities for their application. To use the images professionally, you need permission from V&A Images, as the V&A controls – on behalf of others – the rights held in its books and CD-Roms. *V&A Pattern* can only ever be a tiny selection of the designs available at www.vandaimages.com. We see requests to use images as an opportunity to help us to develop and improve our licensing programme – and for us to let you know about images you may not have found elsewhere.

William Morris
and Morris & Co.
Linda Parry

Few British homes have not used Morris designs in one form or another as a revival of interest in William Morris's work developed throughout the second half of the twentieth century. These popular repeating patterns are easy on the eye and possess a timeless quality that sits well with the fashions of our age. They are also a reminder of the joys of the British countryside and have a modern appeal surprising in work created over 120 years ago.

William Morris (1834–1896) began designing patterns for his own use, but he also wanted to improve the general standards of decorative design in Britain – and the conditions of manufacture. This desire led him to establish his own workshops, first in Queen Square in central London and then from 1881 at Merton Abbey near Wimbledon in south London. Morris & Co. designed not only home interiors, but also a wide range of products for the home, including stained-glass windows, furniture, decorated tiles, printed and woven textile furnishings, carpets and tapestries. Wallpapers were made for the firm by Jeffrey & Co., a leading nineteenth-century London manufacturer and sold exclusively in Britain in the Morris & Co. shop in Oxford Street and through agents in major cities throughout Europe, America and Australia. Repeating designs decorated many of these products and the company's popularity and commercial success was based to a great extent on the artistic skills of William Morris and a small group of other designers working for the company he founded.

Over the extended life of the firm (1861–1940) it was Morris and his assistant, John Henry Dearle (1860–1932), who provided the bulk of the work. After Morris's death, Dearle became chief designer and Artistic Director, helping to extend the firm's commercial success into the twentieth century. But what were the artistic qualities that made Morris & Co. succeed in a very competitive Victorian market? Although Morris was not a natural draughtsman he had a rare talent for creating patterns, seeing them in blocks of colour and not as a series of lines. This skill enabled him, at the height of his career, to create numerous successful designs in swift succession with little apparent effort. His younger daughter, May, referred to it in later years as 'a heaven sent gift'. Getting to this stage was not an easy task, however, and was achieved through hard work and a combination of a wide range of old and new practices and ideas.

Morris insisted on learning how things were made, selecting old manufacturing techniques such as dyeing cloth and yarn with natural plant and animal dyes, block printing and hand weaving, that he identified in the objects he admired most from the past. He also studied traditional pattern formations and systems of repeat, noting which ones worked best for each of the techniques he employed. As he became aware of the benefits and limitations of each, he worked with more and more confidence. His research developed into an unusual depth of knowledge and, as a result, he became one of the most respected art historians of his generation, advising institutions including the Victoria and Albert Museum (then called The South Kensington Museum). However, Morris's use of tried and tested ideas from the past only translated into the successful designs we know today because of his careful choice of subjects. Throughout his life he possessed an understanding and a deep love of all natural things – flowers, trees, insects, birds and animals – that gave his designs an authority gained from close observation. His choice of indigenous British flora was highly unusual when he began designing in the 1860s; previously only brightly coloured, exotic, imported blooms were considered the only acceptable floral decoration for the home. Morris chose to use field and hedgerow plants such as columbine, larkspur, fritillary, jasmine and honeysuckle, with the curving branches of oak, willow and acanthus leaves usually providing the traditional structure in which the flowers would sit.

In 1882 Morris analyzed the art of designing pattern in response to a government run commission on art and design. 'On the whole,' he wrote, 'one must suppose that beauty is a marketable quality and that the better the work is all round, as works of art and in its technique, the most likely it is to find favour with the public'. This simple analysis accurately describes what he and his company had achieved. He not only raised the status of British design throughout the commercial world, but he also provided a model for others to follow.

1
William Morris/Morris & Co.
Tulip and Willow textile. Block-printed cotton. UK, 1873 (V&A: CIRC.91–1933)

2
William Morris/Morris & Co.
Tulip textile. Block-printed cotton. UK, 1875 (V&A: T.628–1919)

3
John Henry Dearle/Morris & Co.
Daffodil wallpaper. Block-printed paper. UK, 1903 (V&A: E.1419 –1979)

4
Kate Faulkner/Morris & Co.
Blossom wallpaper. Block-printed paper. UK, 1885 (V&A: E.1427–1979)

5
William Morris/Morris & Co.
Larkspur textile (see also plate 50). Block-printed silk. UK, 1875 (V&A: CIRC.493–1965)

6
William Morris/Morris & Co.
Honeysuckle textile. Block-printed cotton. UK, 1876 (V&A: CIRC.196–1934)

7
William Morris/Morris & Co.
Bird and Anemone textile. Block-printed cotton. UK, before 1881 (V&A: T.654–1919)

8
William Morris/Morris & Co.
Brother Rabbit textile. Block-printed cotton. UK, 1882 (V&A: T.647–1919)

9
William Morris/Morris & Co.
Windrush textile. Block-printed cotton. UK, 1883 (V&A: T.617–1919)

10
William Morris/Morris & Co.
Wey textile. Block-printed cotton. UK, c.1883 (V&A: T.49 –1912)

11
William Morris/Morris & Co.
Kennet textile. Block-printed cotton. UK, 1883 (V&A: T.48 –1912)

12
William Morris/Morris & Co.
Strawberry Thief textile. Block-printed cotton. UK, 1883 (V&A: T.586 –1919)

13
William Morris/Morris & Co.
Lodden textile. Block-printed cotton. UK, 1884 (V&A: T.39–1919)

14
William Morris/Morris & Co.
Rose textile. Block-printed cotton. UK, 1883 (V&A: CIRC.43–1954)

15
William Morris/Morris & Co.
Corncockle textile. Block-printed cotton. UK, 1883 (V&A: CIRC.87–1953)

16
William Morris/The Merton Abbey Workshop.
Cray textile. Block-printed cotton. UK, 1884 (V&A: CIRC.82–1953)

17
William Morris/Morris & Co.
Garden Tulip wallpaper (see also plate 18). Block-printed paper. UK, 1885 (V&A: E.552–1919)

18
William Morris/Morris & Co.
Garden Tulip wallpaper (see also plate 17). Block-printed paper. UK, 1885 (V&A: E.550–1919)

19
William Morris/Morris & Co.
Bower wallpaper. Block-printed paper. UK, 1877 (V&A: E.509–1919)

20
John Henry Dearle/Morris & Co.
Sweet Briar wallpaper. Block-printed paper. UK, 1912 (V&A: E.1405–1979)

21
William Morris/Morris & Co.
Norwich wallpaper. Block-printed paper. UK, 1889 (V&A: CIRC.26–1954)

22
John Henry Dearle/Morris & Co.
Iris wallpaper. Block-printed paper. UK, 1888 (V&A: E.642–1919)

23
William Morris/Morris & Co.
Grafton wallpaper. Block-printed paper. UK, 1883 (V&A: E.533–1919)

24
William Morris/Morris & Co.
Rose wallpaper. Block-printed paper. UK, 1877 (V&A: E.502–1919)

25
William Morris/Morris & Co.
Trellis wallpaper. Block-printed paper. UK, 1864 (V&A: E.452–1919)

26
William Morris/Morris & Co.
Jasmine Trellis textile. Block-printed cotton. UK, 1868–70 (V&A: CIRC.105–1966)

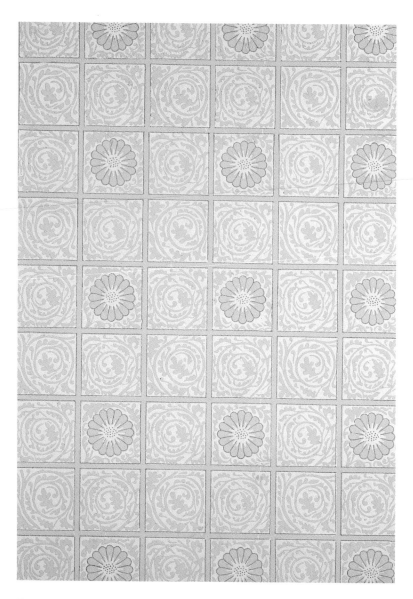

27
William Morris/ Morris & Co.
Diaper wallpaper. Block-printed paper. UK, 1868–70 (V&A: E.458–1919)

28
John Henry Dearle/Morris & Co.
Celandine wallpaper. Block-printed paper. UK, *c.*1896 (V&A: E.2213–1913)

29
William Morris/Morris & Co.
Pink and Rose wallpaper. Block-printed paper. UK, *c.*1890 (V&A: E.581–1919)

30
William Morris/Morris & Co.
Wandle textile. Block-printed cotton. UK, 1884 (V&A: CIRC.427–1953)

31
William Morris/Morris & Co.
Poppy wallpaper. Block-printed paper. UK, 1880 (V&A: E.521–1919)

32
John Henry Dearle/Morris & Co.
The Oak Tree wallpaper. Block-printed paper. UK, 1896 (V&A: E.729–1915)

33
John Henry Dearle/Morris & Co.
Foliage wallpaper. Block-printed paper. UK 1899 (V&A: E.1421–1979)

34
John Henry Dearle/Morris & Co.
Michaelmas Daisy wallpaper. Block-printed paper. UK, *c.*1912 (V&A: E.1403–1979)

35
William Morris/Morris & Co.
Design for *Acanthus* wallpaper (see also plate 36). Pencil, watercolour and bodycolour. UK, 1874 (V&A: CIRC.297–1955)

36
William Morris/Morris & Co.
Acanthus wallpaper (see also plate 35). Block-printed paper. UK, 1875 (V&A: E.496–1919)

37
William Morris/Morris & Co.
Compton wallpaper (see also plate 38). Block-printed paper. UK, 1896 (V&A: E.2216–1913)

38
William Morris/Morris & Co.
Compton wallpaper (see also plate 37). Block-printed paper. UK, 1896 (V&A: CIRC.290–1959)

39
William Morris/Morris & Co.
Fritillary wallpaper (see also plate 40). Block-printed paper. UK, 1885 (V&A: E.545–1919)

40
William Morris/Morris & Co.
Fritillary wallpaper (see also plate 39). Block-printed paper. UK, 1885 (V&A: E.2211–1913)

41
William Morris/Morris & Co.
Venetian wallpaper. Block-printed paper. UK, *c.*1871 (V&A: E.3717–1927)

42
William Morris/Morris & Co.
Queen Anne wallpaper. Block-printed paper. UK, *c.*1868–70 (V&A: E.3722–1927)

43
William Morris/Morris & Co.
Fruit wallpaper (see also plate 44). Block-printed paper. UK, 1866 (V&A: E.3711–1927)

44
William Morris/Morris & Co.
Fruit wallpaper (see also plate 43). Block-printed paper. UK, 1866 (V&A: E.3712–1927)

45
William Morris/Morris & Co.
Branch wallpaper. Block-printed paper. UK, c.1871 (V&A: E.3699–1927)

46
William Morris/Morris & Co.
Marigold wallpaper. Block-printed paper. UK, 1875 (V&A: CIRC.275–1959)

47
William Morris/Morris & Co.
Vine wallpaper. Block-printed paper. UK, 1874 (V&A: CIRC.278–1959)

48
William Morris/Morris & Co.
Norwich wallpaper. Block-printed paper. UK, 1889 (V&A: CIRC.289–1959)

49
William Morris/Morris & Co.
Lily wallpaper. Block-printed paper. UK, 1874 (V&A: CIRC.276–1959)

50
William Morris/Morris & Co.
Larkspur wallpaper (see also plate 5). Block-printed paper. UK, *c.*1875 (V&A: E.472–1919)

51
William Morris/Morris & Co.
Willow Bough wallpaper. Block-printed paper. UK, 1887 (V&A: CIRC.284–1959)

52
William Morris/Morris & Co.
Acorn wallpaper. Block-printed paper. UK, 1879 (V&A: CIRC.282–1959)

53
William Morris/Morris & Co.
Scroll wallpaper. Block-printed paper. UK, *c*.1871 (V&A: E.639–1915)

54
William Morris/Morris & Co.
Bruges wallpaper. Block-printed paper. UK, 1888 (V&A: CIRC.287–1959)

55
William Morris/Morris & Co.
Chrysanthemum wallpaper. Block-printed paper. UK, 1877 (V&A: E.802–1915)

56
William Morris/Morris & Co.
Daisy wallpaper. Block-printed paper. UK, 1864 (V&A: E.3718–1927)

57
William Morris/Morris & Co.
Apple wallpaper (see also plate 58). Block-printed paper. UK, 1877 (V&A: E.508–1919)

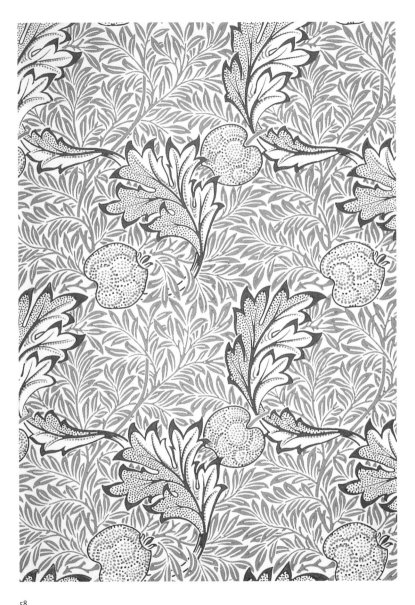

58
William Morris/Morris & Co.
Apple wallpaper (see also plate 57). Block-printed paper. UK, 1877 (V&A: E.506–1919)

59
William Morris/Morris & Co.
St. James' wallpaper. Block-printed paper. UK, 1881 (V&A: E.528–1919)

60
John Henry Dearle/Morris & Co.
Anemone wallpaper. Block-printed paper. UK, 1897 (V&A: E.736–1915)

61
John Henry Dearle/Morris & Co.
Brentwood wallpaper. Block-printed paper. UK, 1913 (V&A: E.1417–1979)

Kate Faulkner/Morris & Co.
Bramble wallpaper. Block-printed paper. UK, 1879 (V&A: E.1414–1979)

63
William Morris/Morris & Co.
Jasmine wallpaper. Block-printed paper. UK, 1872 (V&A: E.770–1915)

64
William Morris/Morris & Co.
Flora wallpaper. Block-printed paper. UK, 1891 (V&A: E.593–1919)

65
William Morris/Morris & Co.
Blackthorn wallpaper. Block-printed paper. UK, 1892 (V&A: E.481–1919)

66
John Henry Dearle/Morris & Co.
Seaweed wallpaper. Block-printed paper. UK, 1901 (V&A: E.1418–1979)

Further Reading

Clark, Fiona
William Morris:
Wallpapers and Chintzes
London, 1973

McCarthy, Fiona
William Morris:
A Life for Our Time
London, new edition 2003

Oman, Charles C,
and Hamilton, Jean
Wallpapers
London, 1982

Parry, Linda, ed.
William Morris
London, 1996

Parry, Linda
Textiles of the Arts &
Crafts Movement
London, new edition 2005

Digital Images

The patterns reproduced in this book are stored on the accompanying compact disc as jpeg files (at approximately A5-size, 300 dpi). You should be able to open them, and manipulate them, direct from the CD-ROM in most modern image software (on Windows or Mac platforms), and no installation should be required (although we, as publishers, cannot guarantee absolutely that the disc will be accessible for every computer).

Instructions for tracing and tiling the images will be found with the documentation for your software.

The names of the files correspond to the V&A inventory numbers of the images.